In Search
of
Love

In Search
of
Love

María Inés
Hitateguy

All scriptural quotations are from the New Standard Bible.

ISBN 10: 1-59298-146-1
ISBN 13: 978-1-59298-146-5
Library of Congress Control Number: 2006902287

Printed in the United States of America
First Printing: April 2006
09   08   07   06   05   6   5   4   3   2   1

drawings by María Inés Hitateguy
cover and layout design: John Toren

Beaver's Pond Press, Inc.
7104 Ohms Lane, Suite 216
Edina, MN 55439-2129
(952) 829-8818
www.BeaversPondPress.com

Beaver's Pond Press, Inc.

Dedication

To my parents, Carlos Hitateguy and Nélida Mignaco de Hitateguy, whom God chose to give me life and who, in spite of their own limitations to give and receive love, worked hard to give me the best they could give. Thank you, Papá. Thank you, Mamá.

Acknowledgments

The process of writing this book has been a wonderfully healing and transforming personal experience. It was also a difficult experience that I could not have done without the prayer and the guidance and support of a number of people.

Thank you Gene and Betty Ofsread for letting me use your cabin where, alone with God, I planned every chapter of this book. Thank you also for your constant support and love.

Thank you Priscilla Herbison, director of the Human Development Program at Saint Mary's University and my advisor, for your guidance, your encouragement of my writing of this book, and your constant motivation.

Thanks to each member of my women's group for allowing me to create a space where in sharing our experiences we learned to grow and allow God's love to heal us.

A special word of thanks to JoAnn Horrisberger for first editing this book, and for making valuable suggestions that helped to make my message clearer and easier to read.

Thank you to all members of Jesus Heals Ministry, especially Bob Schoenecker, for helping me to find the way out of darkness, for your prayers, and spiritual guidance.

Table Of Contents

❧ Introduction

It was the first day of my vacation at a cabin by a lake. The day was beautiful, the sun was shining, and a soft breeze touched my face like a caress from God letting me know of His loving presence. Indeed He was there. He was there in the trees and the flowers. He was there singing for me through the birds. He was there playing with me as I threw the fishing line in the lake, where, suddenly, all the fish seemed to have disappeared. He was there in the calm water of the lake. He was there saying *be still and know I am God.*

The Creator of heaven and earth has been with me all my life, even when I did not know Him and when I did not know He loves me. He was there even when I was afraid of Him. He was always there waiting for me. He touched my heart with His love. Tears run down my cheeks when I ponder my very long journey in search of Love to fill my emptiness.

> *For we are God's handiwork, created in Christ Jesus for the good work that God has prepared in advance, that we should live in them.*
> —Ephesians 2:10

God created me perfect for the work He planned in advance for me to do. He knit me in my mother's womb, and in His book He wrote what I was going to do every day of my life.

I think God planned for me to write this book. I know that God and only God could bring me to where I am. Only He, with His gentle, loving way, could move me spiritually, physically, and emotionally step by step, little by little, from a ranch in the middle of Uruguay to where I am now.

This book is not about my family's problems or my childhood experiences of abuse. I do not seek to hurt in any way the good memory and reputation of my parents, who are no longer in this world. I write this book in the deep belief that God intends for me to use the painful experiences of my life to bring healing and hope to readers who may have experienced physical, emotional, or sexual abuse or who may have grown up in a painful, conflict-ridden environment.

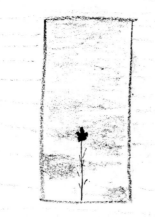

Inside of You

*Inside of you
are the most precious resources.
Because inside of you
God has placed everything you need
to fulfill your destiny.
Inside of you
are the answers to your questions.
Inside of you
is the healing power that heals all wounds.
Inside of you
is the fountain of endless creativity.
Inside of you
is the source of infinite
love, goodness, and peace.
Everything is available to you,
Inside of you*

—María Inés Hitateguy

The kingdom of God is within you.

—Luke 17:21

Seek first the kingdom of God and his righteousness, and all those things will be given to you as well.

—Matthew 6:33

Destiny ✺

The Spirit of the Lord God is upon me, because the Lord has anointed me, He has sent me to bring glad tidings to the lowly, to heal the brokenhearted, to proclaim liberty to the captives and release to the prisoners.

—Isaiah 61:1

I was born on a ranch, in the center of Uruguay. My father, born into the second generation of a Basque family of immigrants from France, worked hard on the land from sunrise to sunset. He was quiet, introverted, and soft-spoken. He loved living and working in the country.

My mother, on the contrary, was a lively and creative city girl, the second generation of an Italian family. She loved to talk, dance, and play. She found life in the country slow and dreary. She taught herself how to sew, and she made most of our clothing until we were young adults. She was also a good cook who could transform leftovers into delicious and attractive dishes. She worked hard and wanted only the best for us: the best education, the best cloth, the best house, and she did her best to keep the family united.

When we lived on the ranch, we had a cook and two maids who helped my mother with the children and the work in the house. My mother taught sewing to women who came from a town nearby. At that time we were six girls and a boy. My youngest brother was born after we moved to the city.

We did not go to church often because the closest church was in a little town a few miles away. The priest came once or twice a month to celebrate mass.

I do remember the little church, but do not recall the priest, the people we met there, or what we, the children, did. I also do not remember if my parents taught us much about God, Jesus, or prayer.

To others outside our home, we appeared to be a good family. We were not. I have since learned the word "dysfunctional." It applies to us. My parents did not have a good marriage. My mother was unhappy and frustrated living in the country. She also wanted to be a teacher, but she could not finish her schooling because of family difficulties with her parents.

Among my fondest memories of childhood are memories of my pets. I had a lamb I called Primavera (Spring) and some horses. I loved to ride early in the morning with my father. My father brought Primavera to my care because her mother died when she was born. I was always feeding her with a big bottle of warm milk from the cows. Very soon she became a round big sheep. When I was in the house and she was hungry, she came into the house looking for me. My mother made me take her out as fast as I could. Primavera, other animals, and nature in general were my comfort and joy during my childhood.

Two childhood experiences painfully affect me even to the present. When I was five years old, I was sexually abused by a man who lived in our house. He had worked with my father and my father's family for a long time, and we considered him part of the family. I never said anything about the abuse to anyone in my family. The abuse continued until I was about seven and was able to stop him from touching me.

At the same time, my parents were having problems with each other. Their problems affected the entire family. One day my parents were taking a nap after lunch, and I was playing in the next room. All of a sudden I heard my father screaming. I ran into their bedroom and saw my father trying to take a gun out of my mother's hand. Somehow I got the gun from my mother's hand, took it outside, and called for help. I never knew what happened between them that day or what my mother intended to do. This was the first time I saw my father so angry and frustrated that he wanted to leave us. After that my father started to drink and eventually became an alcoholic.

I believe that experience paralyzed my emotions and warped my emotional development. For many years I felt like a little child, yet at the same time, I often behaved like an adult. At a very young age, I took responsibility for my siblings' protection to the point that my youngest sister called me "mamá chiquita" (little mom).

Fear and insecurity controlled me for many years. I was always afraid that my mother would try again to kill herself or others and that I would find my parents dead in their bed. Many times I got up two or three times during the night to check on my parents. Each time my father went to town for business or to my uncle's house, I waited for him at the top of the hill overlooking the road. I was afraid he would not come back or that if he did, he would be drunk or would have had an accident.

We had school at home until I was nine years old. We moved to the city when it was time for my oldest brother to attend high school. I was a good, dedicated student and tried hard to be the best. I now know that it was a way for me to please my parents so they would be happy and, at the same time, I would feel good about myself.

During my childhood and teenage years, I imagined God was far away from me. I thought He got angry at me when I did wrong. I believed that in order to be loved and accepted by God, I needed to be "a good girl."

I am sure my parents loved me, but I don't remember ever hearing "I love you" or being hugged. They simply didn't show their love for us or for each other. I only remember one or two times when I saw my parents kissing or hugging each other. Those moments were the happiest for me.

When I went to college I studied to be a teacher, but my dream was to be a doctor. I graduated when I was 20 years old and immediately started my teaching career.

Before I graduated, I met I young man, my first love. I thought we were going to get married after my graduation. I took my first teaching job in a countryside school where I lived for two years. One time I returned to my hometown for a weekend only to find that my fiancée was seeing someone else. This painful experience took me a long time to overcome. The hurt devastated and battered my already low self-esteem and insecurity, consequences of my childhood experiences. After learning of my fiancée's betrayal, I decided to move to Montevideo to work and go to graduate school. I specialized in preschool education and lived and worked in Montevideo until I came to the United States.

Psychology and child psychology were an important part of my college programs, both undergraduate and graduate. I began to understand that what happened to me when I was a child hurt me and deeply affected my life. When I was 26 years old I went to see a psychologist. There, for the first time, I talked about the sexual abuse of my childhood. I went to therapy for about a year and a half. I think it was during those years that I stopped attending church. I still had no relationship with God.

I desperately wanted to be loved, to feel I was important to someone, to know that I did not have to do things for others in order to be recognized and loved. I searched for love in the wrong places, and, without knowing it, I only hurt myself more. In doing so I experienced even more rejection and emotional pain each time that my hope for a new good relationship ended.

Although I revealed my secrets to the psychologist, the abuse continued to be a secret from my family and friends. As a consequence, each time I tried to make new connections, especially with men, I failed and experienced new disconnections.

I came to the United States in January 1979. I learned English, went back to school, and graduated with a degree in business administration and marketing.

The year before I graduated, I received a call from home saying that my father had cancer and had only a few months to live. I went home for Christmas and stayed with my family for a month. Saying goodbye to my father was the most difficult thing I remember ever having to do. For the first time I said, "Te quiero mucho, Papá (I love you very much, Dad)" and he answered, "Yo también te quiero (I love you, too)." Three months later he died.

It was a painful time. I started going to church again. I was sure my father was in heaven and maybe, just maybe, he would speak to me through God. I went to church and just sat there for long time crying and crying, feeling unloved and alone.

After my graduation, I had the opportunity to continue my studies in international business. I moved to Arizona for my master's degree in international management. There I met a group of young adult Christian students who invited me to participate in a prayer and Bible study group. Jesus started His work in me even though I was not really aware of what was going on. For the first time I began to read the Bible. I started to know God as a loving parent.

After completing my master's program, I came back to Saint Paul, Minnesota, and worked in international business until 1994. This was a time of many changes and hard work. I continued to go to church, and I started to participate in church activities and ministries.

One time I got very sick with a stomach ulcer I did not know I had. I was in the hospital for five days to receive blood transfusions. The doctors thought I would die. After I went home from the hospital, one of my coworkers came to see me with a friend from her church. They prayed for me to be filled with the Holy Spirit. I remember I got very hot and started to cry. It was a strange experience.

After two weeks I went to see my doctor. He was surprised to see how well I was. Tests showed my stomach had completely healed! "It looks like you never had a problem in your stomach," said the doctor.

The God I was starting to know loved me. He had a plan for me and a purpose for me to fulfill.

> *For I know well the plans I have in mind for you,*
> *says the Lord, plans for your welfare, not for woe!*
> *Plans to give you a future full of hope.*
> – Jeremiah 29:11

I went back to work in the spring as new leaves appeared on the trees. Pointing to a tree outside our office window, I said to one of my coworkers, "Look how beautiful that tree is." She looked at me like I was crazy and said, "I see nothing different with that tree." But I could see! Nature's beauty is a remainder of God's presence and His gift of comfort, joy, and love for me.

Through my work in international business I met Darin (not his real name). We fell in love. He was my friend, my partner in the business, and my husband to be, or so I thought. We had our future planned. We worked hard many hours a day. He traveled everywhere for business. One day he went to close a transaction, and I never saw him or heard from him again.

❧ Destruction or stepping stones?

For several months after Darin disappeared, I cried and begged God to send him back. I desperately wanted to know what happened, but I was not giving God the opportunity to answer. I felt it was the end of my life. I was emotionally and financially broke. I felt I had no more strength. I did not know where to go or what to do with my life. One day I heard of Jesus Heals Ministry, a group of people whose ministry was, and still is, to pray for healing in the gifts and power of the Holy Spirit. I met with them once or twice a week. They became my friends and my support for everything. There, I met Jesus again as if for the first time. It was indeed the beginning of a new life. I started my journey with the Lord in a new way. He began to heal me, going deeper and deeper into my heart, my memories, my whole being. He got to the place in me where I had buried the pain of my childhood years: the shame, darkness, fear, rejection, low self-esteem, condemnation, negativism, and more. I had pushed those memories so deep inside of me for so many years that it was very difficult to bring everything to the surface. Jesus took it all with Him, little by little. From glory to glory, He set me free. He gave me His love and His peace, a love and peace no one can take away from me.

> *Once you were forsaken, hated and unvisited, now I will make you the pride of the ages, a joy to generation after generation. You shall suck the milk of nations, and be nursed at royal breasts; you shall know that I, the Lord, am your savior, your redeemer, the Mighty one of Jacob. In place of bronze I will bring gold, instead of iron, silver; in place of wood, bronze, instead of stones, iron; I will appoint peace your governor, and justice your ruler. No longer shall violence be heard of in your land, or plunder and ruin within your boundaries. You shall call your walls "Salvation" and your gates "Praise." No longer shall the sun be your light by day, nor the brightness of the moon shine upon you at night. The Lord shall be your light forever, your God shall be your glory. No longer shall your sun go down, or your moon withdraw, for the Lord will be your light forever and the days of your mourning shall be at an end.*
> — Isaiah 60:15-20

At the time Darin disappeared, it never crossed my mind that this very experience of loss, pain, loneliness, and despair was actually the first stepping stone that guided me in the right direction in my search for true love.

My emptiness, sadness, and loneliness brought me to participate more in the church and to help people from the Hispanic community in any way I could.

I started to make new connections and new friends. One day I called my mother in Uruguay and we had a good talk. For the first time she told me she loved me and wanted very much to see me again. For the first time I was able to honestly say to her, "I love you." I felt in my heart I had forgiven her. Instead of resentment and anger, I had love and compassion for her. I reconnected with her and with my family. Two weeks later Mom suffered a heart attack and died in her sleep.

It was a new loss, a new stepping stone to a new stage. I felt discouraged and tired, yet I was learning to hear God's gentle voice saying, "My grace is sufficient."

God knows how much we can handle. When we think we have no more strength to go on, He refreshes us. He tells us,

> *Fear not, for I have redeemed you; I have called you by name: you are mine. When you pass through the water, I will be with you; in the rivers you shall not drown. When you walk through the fire, you shall not be burned; the flames shall not consume you.*
>
> *For I am the Lord, your God, the Holy One of Israel, your Savior.*
>
> — Isaiah 43:1-3

For about two years, I did not have a steady job. To support myself I started to paint clothing and make crafts to sell. For me, this creativity was more than a source of income; it was a therapy. I spent many hours painting and listening to music.

Surrender ✤

Commit your ways to the Lord, trust in him and He will do this.

> – Psalm 37:5

Until one is committed there is hesitancy, the chance to draw back, always ineffectiveness ... Boldness has genius, power, and magic in it. Begin it now.

> – Goethe

After years of searching, healing, and changing, I learned that if I want stability in my life, then I must surrender my life to God. To surrender is to give oneself up or over to the power of another.

I cannot give myself so completely unless I trust the situation or the person, even when the One I surrender to is God. Surrendering to God, then, begins with trust. Trust begins with knowledge, understanding, and faith in God's mercy and love.

The sexual abuse in my childhood created in me a false trust. In my desire for love, confidence, and security, I pretended to trust others to establish relationships with them. My trust was a façade. Inside of me, I built big walls of protection, not allowing others to know me. I was always, unconsciously, testing the other person's intentions and actions. I did not realize what I was doing, so I often felt used, rejected, and hurt.

To surrender my life to God, first I needed to know and trust God. I needed to absolutely and completely know that God loves me, to know that God is Love. Love is His nature and, if He is Love, then everything He has for me is out of His love for me. I have to know He formed me in my mother's womb; He made me perfect for the purpose He has for me.

> *You formed my inmost being; you knit me my mother's womb.*
>
> – Psalm 139:13

Yet I could not know that God loves me because I did not know what love felt like. How could I trust God or any one, when trusted people in my innocent childhood years had used me, hurt me, and abused me? If I could not trust God and did not know of His faithful, true love for me, then how could I entrust my life to Him so completely?

No one can
do it for you ✤

Knowing God is a personal decision. It takes commitment and it requires spending time with Him in prayer, meditation, and reflection. Many times people told me, "Maria, God wants you to seek first His Kingdom and His righteousness and everything will be given to you" (Matthew 6:33). I did not understand what they were telling me. I was going to church on Sunday, I was trying to lead a decent life, and I always tried to help others. What else did God want me to do? I did not know that the Kingdom of God is within me. The Kingdom of God, says God's Word, is within me (Luke 17:21). I had to find the God in me. I had to allow God to work in me and flow through me.

To let God work in me I had to let go of everything that is not of God in my life. Only after I let God do the work in me—and only He knows what needed to be done—was I able to honestly start my journey with God to find, know, and understand my true self. To find the person God created in His image to be loved and to love, to live in peace and to enjoy the life God Himself had planned before I was born, I had to let God do His work in me.

I had to believe that "greater is He Who is in me than he who is in the world" (I John 4:4). I had to believe that God knows how much I could bear. I just had to believe that God loves me. The decision was mine. No one could do it for me. No one can do it for you.

Seeing and accepting what I found inside myself was not easy. The decision to let God into your heart, to receive His love and to trust Him and let Him do the work He knows needs to be done in you, is a personal decision. He promised He will finish the work He begins in us. He promised He will never leave us (Isaiah 43:1-5).

I said "yes" to Him. I invited Him into my heart, but it was not a complete surrender. It was only a beginning.

Until we surrender all to God we continue to struggle, because He wants all of us, all of our life. He wants our past, our present, and our future. We cannot say "I give you this much of me, but not the rest."

If you are struggling with something in your life, then let me ask you, why have you not allowed Jesus's light to touch you? The truth will set you free. The truth is that God loves you so much that if you had been the only person in the whole universe, then Jesus still would have died on the cross. He still would have died for you. God loves each one of His children that much.

Look what is ahead, said the Lord.
Stay still and you will see.
You will see the storm pass away
and the sky clearing up.
I thank the Lord for the new thing He has for me.
I do not see it yet, but I know it is there.
Oh yes now I see.
The turning point is my trust in Him.
Here I am, Lord
I do want to do your will.

– María Inés Hitateguy

❦ Love and the absence of Love

*I give you a new commandment: Love one another.
As I have love you so you also should love one
another. This is how all will know that you are
my disciples, if you have love for one another.*

– John 13:34-35

*The best and most beautiful thing in the world
cannot be seen or even heard, but must be felt with
the heart.*

– Helen Keller

According to research by mental health profession-
als, a lack of love and emotional support from parents
during one's childhood is the main cause of emotional
problems in one's adult life. However, the same research tells us that children who grow up in dysfunctional families or in less-than-nurturing environments
are not destined to be emotionally unstable adults.

We do not need to carry childhood pain all our
lives, nor should we feel guilty all our lives when we
didn't raise our children in a perfect environment.
Adults have the capacity to make decisions and to
choose what to do with painful experiences. We can
use these experiences for our benefit and the benefit of

others, or we can let them destroy our life and the lives of those around us.

During my healing and searching, I felt sick again. My doctor found a large ominous mass in my uterus. I had three large, benign, fast-growing tumors. I learned that many women with similar uterine tumors were sexually abused as children. Since I had grown in my personal relationship with God, and since I believed that some illnesses have roots in emotional problems, I trusted God for healing. He healed me again.

I attended a conference at which a priest talked about healing our memories. After he talked, he prayed for the audience. He prayed for the women who were sexually abused as children. I felt he was praying directly for me. I started crying and, again, a heat covered me completely. After this prayer, he invited people with specific needs to approach him for individual prayer. On my turn, I told him I was one of the women abused as a child. He started praying in tongues. The priest said "God wants you to receive His love." The Lord was saying, "Receive my love, María, My love will set you free." I said, "I do not know how." For the first time I understood the root of my problems: I never felt loved. With the help of the priest, I was able to overcome the painful emptiness I felt deep inside of me and to say, "Lord, I do want to receive Your Love. I do want to be loved, please help me."

God's love penetrated my mind, body, and spirit completely. I felt that Jesus took all my pain, rejections, insecurity, and shame, and He canceled them on the cross once and for all. Many times I heard and read: *"For God so loved the world that He sent His only Son, so everyone who believes in Him might not perish but might have eternal life"* (John 3:16). Now I understood.

I later understood that God was saying to me what He said to Jesus the day He was baptized: *"You are my beloved son; with you I am well pleased"* (Luke 3:22). "You are my beloved daughter, María; with you I am well pleased."

I thought God's love for "the world" meant other people, not me. Now I know I am the world God loves so much. Now I know that if I would have been the only person in the face of the earth Jesus still would have died for me. There is no greater love than this.

> *Yet it was our infirmities that He bore, our sufferings that He endured, while we thought of Him as stricken, as one smitten by God and afflicted. But He was pierced for our offenses, crushed for our sins. Upon Him was the chastisement that makes us whole, by His stripes we were healed.*
>
> – Isaiah 54:4-5

After the prayer I went home and fell asleep. When I woke up the next morning, my tummy was flat. I had no discomfort. The tumors had disappeared. I felt more happy and peaceful than ever before. Everyone asked me, "What happened to you? You look different." I certainly was different. God's love healed me, and He stayed with me forever.

I want to tell everyone that what God did for me, He can do for others too. Knowing and receiving God's love for me did not automatically change my life or remove the painful memories of the past. Yet His love gave me the strength and the faith I needed to go through the change process. Change requires time, patience, and commitment to God's principles and to God's way of working with us. Working with God in this process of change helped me to acknowledge the negative and repressed feelings I held. With God's help and love, I changed and healed my unwanted behaviors: people-pleasing to get recognition and acceptance, repressed anger, fear of authority figures, frozen emotions, overdeveloped sense of responsibility, and the need to take of care others to feel valuable. I learned that what I often did for others—thinking I was caring for those I loved—was not truly love but was instead a way to fill my own emptiness and loneliness. I learned that I cannot give what I don't have. I cannot truly love others without first receiving God's love for me.

> *If I speak in human and angelic tongues but do not have love, I am a resounding gong or a clashing cymbal.*
> — 1 Corinthians 13:1

When I was a child, I thought that God loved me when I was good and punished me when I was not good. Now I know that God's love is unconditional. God wants always to bless us with His love, His joy, and His peace. God's love for me is based in what He is. And He is Love. God's love for me does not depend on what I deserve or do not deserve. Even when I need to be loved by another person, my happiness and peace are not conditional on what I receive from others. I do not have to do things for others to be loved by others.

> *For I am convinced that neither death, nor life, nor angels, nor principalities, nor present things, nor future things, nor powers, nor height, nor depth, nor any other creature will be able to separate us from the love of God in Christ Jesus our Lord."*
>
> – Romans 8:38-39

> *But God, Who is rich in mercy, because of the great love He had for us, even when we were dead in our transgressions, brought us to life with Christ, raised up with Him and seated us with Him in the heavens in Christ Jesus.*
>
> – Ephesians 2:4-6

God wants to love me. He has to love me because He is love. I was created in His image, so I was created to love. When my faith in God and in His Word started to grow, I began to heal myself. When I understood and believed that God loves me, I started to accept and love myself. Then I was able to love others without the fear of getting hurt again. This love comes from knowing who I truly am, from a feeling of inner peace, from the ability to give and to receive, and from how much I appreciate others and myself because I know I am a beloved child of God and so are they. This love creates a state of gratitude and compassion, a feeling of connection with God and with others.

I am still learning how to give and receive love. Sometimes my old fears, doubts, and expectations still affect my desire to love and to be loved. When this happens, I have to stop and make a conscious decision to let go of the past and believe, even more, in the power of love. I have to believe that true love produces relationships, healthy care of others and of oneself, freedom, joy, and peace. Love is like a positive energy that helps us in our personal and interpersonal development. Love opens the doors to personal development and vitality.

In giving we receive. The more we give the more we receive. The more I give love, the more I will be loved.

> *Give and it will be given to you. A good measure,*
> *pressed down, shaken together and running over,*
> *will be poured into your lap. For with the measure*
> *you use, it will be measured to you.*
>
> – Luke 6:38

I still had to learn how to receive. I had to learn how to ask for the essence rather than the form of what I want. For example, rather than ask that a specific person love me, I should ask to be loved regardless of the source. To receive love I had to learn to let go of old patterns and to let God make all things new.

> *That you should put away the old self of your*
> *former way of life, corrupted though deceitful*
> *desires, and be constantly renewed in the spirit*

*of your mind, and put on the new self, created in
God's way in righteousness and holiness of truth.*
– Ephesians 5: 22-24

To love is a decision, not a feeling. Similarly,
to forgive is also a decision. We choose to love. We
choose to forgive. We learn to look for the good in
each person. Jesus does this for each one of us and ex-
pects us to do the same.

*For this is the message you have heard from the
beginning: We should love one another.*
– 1 John 4:11

God's commandment was not that we feel love
for one another, but that we love one another. What
God asks us to do is always possible. It is what He had
planned for us from the beginning, even before He created the world.

I do not know my future, but now I know who I
am in Christ. I know the person God created and the
many gifts He gave me. Above all, I know I am loved.
I may not be where I should be or where I would like
to be, but I thank God that I am far away from where
I was.

When I was a child a man destroyed my identity
and self-esteem, but they were restored by Jesus, because even before I knew Him, He had died on the
cross for me. God says in Isaiah 43:4: *"Since you are
precious and honored in my sight, and because I love you, I
will give men in exchange for you and people in exchange for
your life."*

I know that the Lord is God. It is He who made me, and I am His.

— Psalm 100:3

❧ From sorrow to joy

Amen, amen, I say to you, you will weep and mourn, while the world rejoices; you will grieve, but your grief will become joy. When a woman is in labor, she is in anguish because her hour has arrived; but when she has given birth to a child, she no longer remembers the pain because of her joy that a child has been born into the world. So you also are now in anguish. But I will see you again, and your hearts will rejoice, and no one will take your joy away from you.

– John 17:20-23

I worked for a while with pregnant women. These young women believed that they had met the love of their lives. They believed that they loved and were loved. But the moment they found themselves pregnant, the loved one disappeared. These young mothers-to-be came to the program asking for help, desperately wanting to have their loved one back.

One of these women, Jasmine (not her real name), called me from the hospital. It was time for her delivery. When I arrived, she had been in labor for a few hours. The baby was breach and the doctor started to discuss the possibility of a caesarean, which Jasmine did not want. I asked Jasmine if I could massage her back. She agreed. As I massaged her back, I prayed for

God's mercy and love to fill Jasmine. Jasmine started to relax. The next time the nurse came to examine Jasmine, the baby had turned and was in the right position. It was time for delivery. It took only a few minutes for the doctor to take the baby and put her on Jasmine's chest. Jasmine's smile lighted her face. With a tender loving voice she said, "Hola amor, yo soy tu mamá. Que bonita eres. (Hi, my love, I am your mom. How beautiful you are)."

It took only a few moments to transform the mother's pain into joy. What a blessing it was for me to witness this experience.

This event is an example of how we are transformed when we receive God's love. It is His love that transforms our pain into joy, peace, and righteousness. This is Jesus's promise. We see the manifestation of His promise in our life when we do our part.

> *Remain in my love. If you keep My commandment you will remain in My love, just as I have kept My Father's commandment and remain in His love. . . so that My joy might be in you and your joy may be complete.*
>
> – John 15:9-11

I am the vine; you are the branches. Whoever remains in me and I in him will bear much fruit, because without me you can do nothing.

– John 15:5-6

The soul will bring forth fruits exactly in the measure in which the inner life is developed in it. If there is no inner life, however great may be the zeal, the high intention, the hard work, no fruit will come forth.

– Charles de Faucald

Transformation ❧

You have taken off your old self with its practices and have put on the new self, which is being renewed in knowledge in the image of its Creator.

— Colossians 3:9-10

My long journey to discover my true self, the woman whom God created, has not been easy, but I regret nothing. I began by identifying what was in me that was not part of my true self. I had to change the way I thought of myself, others, my life, and the world.

I learned about the connection between body, soul, and spirit. With inner healing came physical healing, more self confidence, and less defensiveness. Healing gave me hope of a brighter future. This feeling of well being permeated all areas of my life.

God promised in Jeremiah 30:17 that He will restore my health and heal my wounds. He did.

My healing, transformation, and restoration did not happen at once. It was a path, a road, a journey that started in a dark place. In that dark place, I felt lonely and full of despair. I began searching for Light. I needed new possibilities, happiness, and peace. *"Forget the former things; do not dwell on the past. See I am doing a new thing! Now it springs up; do you not perceive it? I*

am making a way in the desert, a stream in the wasteland"
(Isaiah 43: 18-19).

Changing jobs was not the answer. Changing
homes was not the answer. Changing cars was not the
answer. Changing places was not the answer. A true
change is a change of one's whole being, body, soul,
and spirit. It happens deep within our being, in that
place where we know the truth. The truth will set you
free (John 8:32).

The truth is that God loves me, He loves you, and
He loves those who hurt you and me. The truth is that
He created us in His own image, and that Jesus died for
me, for you and for all others. The truth is that Jesus
took my sins, the sins of others against me, and every
wound I will ever have in my entire life, nailed them
to the cross, and canceled them forever. It is this truth
that gives me the strength to heal and transform.

> He himself bore our sins in His body upon the
> cross, so that, free from sins, we might live for
> righteousness. By His wound you have been
> healed.
>
> – 1 Peter 2:24

Discovering and understanding my true self ☙

My authentic self is the person God created. I can know my authentic self only by believing in God's word. God is our maker. He is the only one who can tell us who we are. The first thing God tells me is that He made me in His image. Genesis 1:27 says, "God created man in His image; in His image he created him; male and female he created them." And, what God created, He said in Genesis 1:31, "is good." God formed man out of the clay of the ground and blew into his nostrils the breath of life, so man became a living being. God Himself, like a craftsman or an artist, worked the soil to form a human figure. This is our human nature, our body. But God placed His Spirit in that body to give it life. God's Spirit gives us life.

The devil's word attracted Adam and Eve. The serpent devil represents the material world. Adam and Eve disobeyed God because they thought disobedience would lead to a better life. This mistaken belief corrupted their authentic self, and they started to see themselves naked. They became afraid of God.

We all go through life struggling to understand who we are and what our purpose is in this world. We struggle with feelings of emptiness, loneliness, and unhappiness. God's plan for us from the beginning was that we were reconciled and united with Him. We will be, we have, and we do all that God had for us from the beginning, only when we receive the new life Jesus conquered for us with His victory over death (2 Corinthians 5:18-21).

God filled my broken heart with His love, and my sadness and loneliness was turned into joy. I am a child of God (John 1:12-13). I am His heir (Galatians 4: 6-7). The God who created the heavens and the earth is my Father (2 Corinthians 6:18). God formed me in my mother's womb, and before I was even born He wrote a plan for my life (Psalm 139:14-16). I am not a failure; I am more than a conqueror (Romans 8:37). I am special. I have been given special gifts, qualities, and talents (Jeremiah 1:5). There is no fear in me (1 John 4:18).

Although I am now in touch with my authentic self, my true identity, I have had to learn how to live as a loving child of God. This is a process that required time, commitment, and persistence.

To understand myself, I had to go inside of me because it is inside of me that I have the Spirit of God who gives me life, understanding, and guidance. We need to know our whole person. We must know how our body, soul, and spirit are interconnected. We need to discover the root of our adult behavior. We need to know that our present actions and reactions may arise from unfulfilled needs.

Scientific research confirms that psychological and emotional experiences influence physical health because our emotions and thoughts generate biochemical reactions in our body. The interconnectedness of body, soul, and spirit is at the same time affected by the environment around us and, in turn, affects this environment. Psychological and sociological studies show how much the environment influences a person's development. These studies recognize the connection between the inner world of a person and the society or outside world in which the person develops.

❧ Beliefs and values

The environment in which we grow up shapes the way we behave and think, creating beliefs and values that are often stored in our unconscious. Based on these unconscious beliefs, we react to external events, people, organizations, or systems. For example, I grew up in a family where one of the parents was frequently creating conflicts and the other avoiding conflicts and confrontations by not responding or by leaving. In my adult life I often found myself responding to conflict in the same way. These reactions may work in the environment where they were learned, but outside this environment they create misunderstanding and more conflicts. The solution, then, is to know ourselves well, to truly know the person God created, to learn our own internal culture, to discover our unconscious beliefs and values, and to bring them to a conscious level. Knowing how God created each of us for a unique purpose and mission helps us to learn that we are all different. This understanding helps us make the necessary adjustment to create healthy connections. Being part of a multicultural community, both at work and at church, and relating to people who are different, helps me see myself differently and learn more about myself.

I learn the truth of myself when I am open to receive the truth. I can be honest and open when I know I am a beloved child of God.

When I began to understand and appreciate my authentic self, when I started to understand that my thoughts create feelings and feelings generate actions, I started to be more aware of the power of my mind and the thoughts I have in my mind. Then I realized I could consciously change my thoughts, and when I constantly make an effort to control my thoughts and free my mind of negative thoughts, my life began to change.

> Be transformed by the renewing of your mind, then you will be able to test and approve what God's will is—His good, pleasing, and perfect will.
>
> – Romans 12:2

To truly understand ourselves, we must deeply explore our personal beliefs. Beliefs and values create our reality. The beliefs we have affect our life, either creating new opportunities and enriching us or limiting and destroying our opportunities and our self.

Some of our beliefs are known to us, they are accessible to us, they are conscious. Examples: I am a creative person, I believe that true change must come from within. I believe we receive what we give. I believe God is always with me. He guides and protects me.

> On the way of wisdom I direct you, I lead you on a straightforward path. When you walk, your step will not be impeded, and should you run, you will not stumble.
>
> – Proverbs 5:11-12

What do you believe about God? What do you believe about the world, society, and people? What do you believe about yourself and your life?

Our beliefs influence our values, relationships, priorities, and goals. I used to believe that I was shy and could not say what was in my heart because others may not like me. I thought I was not smart enough to carry on a conversation with people who had more education than I had. Without my being conscious of it, going to school and learning became a way to escape from the truth inside of me.

Unconscious beliefs are manifestations of hidden, unexplored, or unresolved psychological issues. An unconscious belief is created when we do not want to deal with something, when we have a "secret" inside.

Most unconscious beliefs arise from experiences early in life. Examples: I am never good enough; I can trust no one; people remember me only when they need me. These beliefs only produce bitterness, resentment, and divisions. When I understood that my value and my worth are in who I am in Jesus, then, and only then, was I able to love and to give regardless of the response I received from others.

Often our problems with others happen because of our internal unconscious beliefs, when we are not aware of why we feel and react the way we do.

Knowing our internal unconscious beliefs and values can help us to be more aware of how we are different from others. Knowing these differences helps us adjust and improve our communication and relationships with others.

Sometimes we avoid exploring deeper and deeper because we are afraid of what we may discover; we are afraid of the reality that it may force us to face. Below is a list of beliefs I held or that I heard from others.

What We Believe:	What God Says:
No one truly loves me.	"For God so loved the world that He gave His only Son, so that everyone who believes in Him must not perish but might have eternal life." (John 3:16)
I am not capable.	"God is able to make every grace abundant for you, so that, in all things, always having all you need, you may have an abundance for every good work." (2 Corinthians 10:8)
It is not worth the effort.	"We know that all things work for good for those who love God, who are called according to His purpose." (Romans 8:28)
It is impossible.	"And He said, 'What is impossible for human beings is possible for God.'" (Luke 18:27)
I can trust no one.	"Blessed is the man who trusts in the Lord, whose hope is the Lord. He is like a tree planted beside the waters that stretches out its roots to the streams: It

What We Believe:	What God Says:
	fears not the heat when it comes; its leaves stay green; in the year of drought it shows no distress, but still bears fruit. (Jeremiah 17:7-8)
It is too difficult. I cannot do it.	*"He said to me 'My grace is sufficient for you, for power is made perfect in weakness.' "* (2 Corinthians 12:9)
I am afraid I will not have enough.	*"My God will supply whatever you need, in accord with His glorious riches in Christ Jesus."* (Phillippians 4:19)
People always take advantage of me.	*"Whoever clings to me I will answer; I will be with them in distress; I will deliver them and give them honor."* (Psalm 91: 14-15)
If I am not in control, they will run over me.	*"Softer than butter is their speech, but war is in their hearts. Smoother than oil are their words, but they are unsheathed swords."* (Psalm 55:22)
I am afraid.	*"For God did not give us a spirit of cowardice but rather of power and love and self-control."* (2 Timothy 1:7)

Such internal, hidden beliefs, rooted in negative experiences, affect the way we react to situations, especially if the situation seems similar to those that created our beliefs. Most of the time these beliefs live in our unconsciousness, and our reaction to specific circumstances seems normal to us. We may perceive that people are controlling or imposing their view on us because they may have a strong personality. Such strength may remind us of a parent or authority figure who has the same personality and who may have hurt, oppressed, disrespected, or abused us in the past. We interpret what we see according to such unconscious beliefs, and we respond defensively according to what we have implicitly learned. At the same time, the people we are engaging, not knowing what caused our reaction, may feel hurt or rejected or misunderstood because their perception of the situation is different. Also, of course, our reaction may specifically affect other people because of their unconscious beliefs.

Discovering our unconscious beliefs and bringing them to a conscious level is a lifelong process. This process is an important part of our healing and our personal and interpersonal development.

❧ The power of secrecy

Secrets, family secrets as well as personal secrets, affect our decisions, our behavior and, most of all, our relationships.

No one in my family ever knew of the abuse I suffered when I was five and six years old. I was afraid of my parent's reactions. Quietly and afraid, I tried to do everything my mother asked me to do. Most of the time when I played, I played the role of mother, teacher, or doctor. I took responsibility for my siblings' protection. To protect them, I needed to be in control. Unconsciously, I developed and internalized these behaviors. I denied my needs and my wants to please others because I felt unworthy of receiving care and love. Repeating this behavior to please others became so natural that when I grew up, I continued to act in the same way. I became a people pleaser.

I pleased others to receive their recognition. I might have felt good for a moment, but in the end I felt used, abused, or worn out. I had no peace and no joy. I was doing good out of what my flesh needed in order to feel worthy, but I was not acting out of my authentic self, nor was I seeking guidance from the Holy Spirit.

Secrets influence our relationships because, in an effort to keep the secret out of the relationship, we cannot be authentic. Sometimes at the beginning of a relationship, we do things or allow things to happen knowing that they are not right or clear. Still we allow them because we fear losing the relationship. Most of the time, if a relationship begins this way, it ends in disappointment. Disappointments hurt and create new disconnections. We feel lonely and psychologically isolated. These feelings are very destructive for a person because they interfere with the person's ability to see reality completely and clearly. Unhealed hurts often lead a person to destructive behaviors. Alcoholism, drug addiction, workaholism, eating disorders, gambling, excessive shopping, and so on are addictions unconsciously developed to hide a hurt or a secret. Self-destructive behaviors cover our pain. In the effort to hide the hurt or the secret, the person develops protective behaviors that later become habits. The constant effort of the body to resolve the problems caused by hurting memories sometimes causes physical, mental, or emotional illnesses.

We need to know who we really are. To know who we really are, we must look to our Creator and see in His Words how He created and re-created us in Jesus Christ, our Lord and Savior. When we know who we are in Christ and with Christ, we can face our past and give it to Him to heal, transform, and restore.

Part of the healing process requires us to identify the darkness and to reexperience and grieve our pain. We can go through this process knowing we are loved. Jesus our Way and our Light, will never leave us.

❦ Naming, understanding and breaking the darkness

Inner hurts feel like stepping on slivers of glass. With each step the slivers drive deeper and deeper under the skin. Unless we stop and look for what is causing the pain and remove it, our foot may become infected, swollen, and painful. To remove the shards, we may have to cut some flesh. Although cutting hurts, we will be able to remove the glass, release the pain, and walk again normally.

Emotional hurts are the same. We must stop and search for the root of the hurt, name it, and ask God to heal it.

The process of recognizing the unhealthy behaviors and the roots of these behaviors in my life was not easy, but I regret nothing. With God all things are possible (Mark 10:27).

> *The God of all grace Who calls you to His eternal glory through Christ Jesus will Himself restore, confirm, strengthen, and establish you after you have suffered a little.*
>
> – 1 Peter 5:10

If we ignore our self-destructive behaviors, we will continue to experience struggles and restlessness in our life. As long as we keep the secret, the resentment, or the memory of the hurt alive, we remain in bondage with fear, insecurity, loneliness, rejection, and more. But when we trust God and let Him love us, He will help us bring the secret to the Light Who is Jesus (John 8:12). He will send into our life godly people who will support, listen to, and pray for and with us.

Through prayer for inner healing, the power of the resurrected Jesus Christ enters into our being, mind, body, and spirit, touching and bringing the painful memories into the Light.

> *I am the Light of the world. Whoever follows me will not walk in darkness, but will have the light of life.*
>
> – John 8:12

❧ Breaking the darkness

In the world you will have trouble, but take courage, I have conquered the world.

– John 16:33

When everything in my life seemed wrong and I was tired of trying and trying, I talked with an elderly priest. Crying, I said to him "Is it ever going to end?" I was referring to the many problems in my life. In a peaceful, compassionate voice he just replied, "No." This was certainly not the answer I wanted to hear. Seeing my discouragement, he continued saying, "Not as long as you live in this world, but you don't have to be trapped by the darkness of the world."

How then do we, I, get "un-trapped"? Many years passed before I understood the priest's answer. Jesus said, "In the world you will have trouble, but take courage, I have conquered the world." He teaches us that it is only with Him that we can also overcome the darkness of this world. He is the Way. He is the Truth. He is the Light. "Follow me," Jesus said. Jesus is the answer to all our problems. Jesus releases us from the darkness of this world. With Him, remaining focused and not letting the things of this world distract us from Him, we can live in God's presence. His light and His love nurture and guide us. This is what it means to surrender and trust God, to let yourself be led to new places by the Lord, who calls each one of us "my beloved."

✿ The darkness of fear

Be brave and steadfast; have no fear or dread of them, for it is the Lord, your God, who marches with you; he will never fail you or forsake you.
— Deuteronomy 31:6

Fear paralyzes us. It stops us from doing what God is calling us to do. Fear causes us to miss the blessings God has for us. Fear steals our peace and our joy.

The two frightening episodes of my childhood cast dark clouds over my life. I was afraid that my parents would find out about the abuse; I was afraid that my mother would again try to hurt herself or someone else. I was afraid of the man who abused me. I was afraid of what could happen to my father after he started drinking. I was afraid each time my parents got into a discussion.

I realize now that I grew up in fear. Fear controlled my life. I felt responsible for protecting not only myself but also my sisters and brothers. In order to do that, I developed protective behaviors that created feelings of insecurity.

From the outside I seem brave, smart, and calm, but deep in me the opposite seems true. I did not realize that to avoid being hurt, I built walls of protection and convinced myself that everything was all right. In doing so, I avoided reality instead of confronting it. Confrontation is very difficult for me. Confrontation makes me anxious. I also have trouble seeing reality because I have trouble seeing the whole picture in a particular situation. Instead, I tend to concentrate on details and "what ifs." As a result, I see fragments and slices of reality that seem neither real nor accurate. And because I do not "see" well, I become afraid. This vicious cycle is itself frightening and dark.

When we feel the darkness of fear overwhelming us, we need to stop, turn to the Light and hear Jesus's soft voice saying, "I am with you. I will never leave you. I will never forsake you." Then, we can proceed unafraid. We can trust that whatever the outcome, even when things do not happen the way we would like them to, the results will turn out for our good.

Faith, prayers, and the knowledge, memorization, and internalization of God's word have helped me to overcome fear.

> *Do not be afraid any longer, little flock, for your*
> *Father is pleased to give you the kingdom.*
>   – Luke 12:32

> *And do not be afraid of those who kill the body but*
> *cannot kill the soul.*
>   – Matthew 10:28

> *Fear not, I am with you; be not dismayed; I am*
> *your God. I will strengthen you, and help you, and*
> *uphold you with my right hand of justice.*
>   – Isaiah 41:10

For God did not give us a spirit of cowardice but rather of power and love and self-control.

– 2 Timothy 1:7

The darkness of insecurity ❧

Growing up with fear and secrets, I became insecure and ashamed. These feeling affected my personality, my opinion of myself, and my health. Feelings of shame and insecurity did not disappear in my adult life nor did the physical manifestation of illness disappear. Shame made me also believe that something was wrong with me and that everyone could see it except me. I felt lonely and sad. Not only did I keep these feelings to myself, but also I pretended and acted as though they were not real. In order for me to be able to work through these feelings, I started to do things to perfection. If I invited friends to my house, then I cleaned the house until it shined; I spent hours preparing the meal; I labored to make sure the table and all else looked perfect, the best I could possibly offer.

It took me almost 50 years of my life to understand what I was doing and why. It was only when I received Jesus in my heart and started to read the Bible that I learned that my value and my security is in knowing who I am in Jesus Christ. Then, God started to heal me and set me free from insecurity and shame.

> *Blessed be the God and Father of our Lord Jesus Christ, who in His great mercy gave us new birth to a living hope through the resurrection of Jesus Christ from the dead, to an inheritance that is imperishable, undefiled, and unfading, kept*

*in heaven for you who by the power of God are
safeguarded through faith, to a salvation that is
ready to be revealed in the final time.*

– 1 Peter 1:1-6

Many darknesses affect me and others: the darkness of loneliness, the darkness of sadness and grief, the darkness of rejection, and so on. However, the solution to darkness is to come to the Light, to Jesus Christ, who came to this world so we can have life abundantly.

Healing, transformation, and restoration will differ from person to person, but the answer always appears in God's Word. We are God's beloved children, He formed us perfectly for the purpose and mission for which He created us. We must make a firm decision and commitment to find the true person God created and to follow Jesus' example of how to live, work, and be in God's will.

The darkness of the world will keep pulling at us. Resentment, lack of forgiveness, painful memories, rejection, abuse, jealousy, revenge, greed, and more are part of the darkness of the world. This darkness works in our minds and in our hearts, in our thoughts and feelings. To get away from the pain created by these thoughts and feelings, we avoid or ignore them, telling ourselves we are too busy to face the truth. It takes commitment and persistence to break away from the darkness and walk into the Light. Yet if our heart is right and we honestly want to follow Jesus, then He is faithful and will help us through. The darkness disappears with the Light and our mind and heart will be filled with love, peace, joy, forgiveness, and hope.

Then we can hear the voice of our Heavenly Father saying, "*With age-old love I have loved you; so I have kept my mercy toward you. Again I will restore you, and you shall be rebuilt*" (Jeremiah 31:3).

✿ My experience of inner healing

In the next few pages I address my personal experience of inner healing. Although God works in different ways with different individuals, I believe that there are steps in the healing process that we all go through.

FORGIVENESS

Forgiveness is the beginning of inner and physical healing. Forgiveness is a gift from God. It is free to all who believe. Our part is to ask for forgiveness and to receive it. We must forgive ourselves and forgive others who have sinned against us. *"Forgive and you will be forgiven"* (Luke 6:37).

> *When you stand to pray, forgive anyone against whom you have a grievance, so that your heavenly Father may in turn forgive you your transgressions.*
>
> – Mark 11:25

Forgiveness is for our own good. When we forgive, we break chains of bondage. Forgiveness sets us free and frees the person who hurt us so that the Lord can begin His work in us.

Lack of forgiveness is like poison in our heart. It produces rotten fruits in our life: resentment, conflict, negativism, frustration, and more.

Often we cannot forgive with our own strength alone. Forgiveness is a decision we make: we bring it to the Lord and ask Him to help us to forgive. Every day, sometimes every moment of our life, we have to forgive someone for something. Forgiveness is not a feeling—the feeling will come later. I cannot wait until I feel good, at peace, or strong to say "I forgive you." My experience is that once I make the decision to forgive and I pray for the person I need to forgive, God will give me the grace to forgive. Then I feel peace and the memories of what caused me the pain will have no power over me. Forgiveness gives us the freedom to receive God's love, and God's love heals us.

When we find ourselves struggling with forgiveness, we must remember that there is nothing in this world that Jesus did not suffer first. Jesus was betrayed and abandoned by His friends. He was humiliated, rejected, and unjustly condemned like the worst criminal. He bore all pain for the love of the Father Who calls Him as He now calls us, my beloved. After He was crucified, Jesus said *"Father, forgive them, they know not what they do"* (Luke 23:34).

When we believe what Jesus did for us and receive His gift of salvation and redemption, we allow Jesus to enter in our self and show us the truth of who we are.

In love He destined us for adoption to himself through Jesus Christ, in accord with the favor of His will, for the praise of glory of His grace that He granted us in the Beloved.

– Ephesians 1:5-6

In Him we have redemption by His blood, the forgiveness of transgression, in accord with the riches of His grace that He lavished upon us.

– Ephesians 1:7

When we believe in who we are in Jesus Christ and receive the truth of our identity, everything that is not of God has to go from our life. Jesus gives us the strength and courage we need to allow Him to do the work in us that He needs to do.

The plant needs good soil, water, and sun to transform the seed into a plant that later gives flower and fruits. The soil, water, and sun for our inner transformation are prayer, reading, and meditating on God's Word and giving obedience to God's Word and God's will. We must make time to be in His presence.

All of us, gazing with unveiled face on the glory of the Lord, are being transformed into the same image from glory to glory, as from the Lord who is the Spirit.

– 2 Corinthians 3:18

Prayer helps a person to become one with God. In the strength of our connection with God, we too, like the plants, start to give fruits: love, joy, peace, patience, kindness, generosity, faithfulness, gentleness, and self-control.

Challenges will not disappear from our life, but when our trust is in the Lord, when our eyes are fixed on the God who made heaven and earth, then we can be sure that He will help us through. He will bring us closer and closer to Him. With Him and in Him, we obtain victory. He may not always give us everything we ask for in the way we want to receive it, but we know that everything coming from God is the best for us. When we endure the trial and tribulations, we may not see the good.

I walk by faith one day at a time. I do not know where I am going but knowing the One with whom I walk, my Creator, the source of Love and Light, gives me confidence in the journey. Like the seed that grows from the darkness of the soil into the light of the sun, so we change. We grow from the darkness of our pain, disappointments, rejections, failures, and losses.

This is how I changed from despair to peace, from sadness to joy, from resentment to forgiveness, from hate to love, from confusion to order, and from darkness to light.

> *Therefore, neither the one who plants nor the one who waters is anything, but God, Who causes the growth. The one who plants and the one who waters are equals, and each will receive wages in proportion to his labor. For we are God's coworkers; you are God's field, God's building.*
> – 1 Corinthians 3:7-8

❧ Trust

As I began my healing process, the Lord spoke to me, "You must drink of this cup; you must be crucified." His words passed through my heart like an arrow. There was already too much pain in me and the thought of the cup and cross was more than I was able to understand and accept. I cried to the Lord, "Please no more pain; I can bear no more."

Twelve years later, as I waited in prayer for the result of a biopsy and feared the possibility of being the fourth in my family to face breast cancer, again I heard the Lord say "You must drink of this cup; you must be crucified." All these years the Lord was preparing me to understand His word. It was now time to test my understanding and my response. Jesus' love and peace filled my heart as I responded, "Do with me what you will, your way not mine."

As I share my experience with friends, the reaction from some of them helped me to reaffirm my complete surrender to the Lord. "God wants to heal you," someone said, "We will pray and by faith we know He heals you."

Although it is God's will that His children will be strong, healthy, and happy, we do not know how or when He heals us. What I absolutely know is that whatever God asks me to do, He will help me do and that He will protect me from whatever is not of God. I know God loves me and is always with me. I am in God's hands, and I am at peace. Everything will be for His glory, and He will use it for my good.

The following few weeks, through surgery and recovery, God's presence and peace were very real in me and around me. I received many phone calls from family, friends, and coworkers saying, "I am praying for you" or "You are in my thoughts and my prayers". I felt as if heaven and earth were united in prayer. What a blessing for me to witness that so many people, Christians from many different denominations, as well as non-Christians, recognized the power of prayer and the cry for help to the One God Who invites us to be one in His Love. Jesus prayed to the Father, *"I pray, not only for them, but also for those who will believe in me through their word, so that they may all be one, as you, Father, are in me and I in you, that they also be in us"* (John 17:21).

⚜ What is the cup I must drink? How am I to be crucified?

When, in Matthew 20:22, Jesus asked John and James, "Can you drink the cup I am going to drink?" they instantly said, "Yes, we can," because they did not understand Jesus' question.

The first time Jesus asked me the same question, I did not answer yes or no. I just cried to the Lord not to allow more pain in my life. Now I am in a different place in my relationship with the Lord. I know Him personally. I have experienced the healing power of His love several times before. I now know He is my Lord, my Savior, and my deliverer in whom I trust.

The cup He asked me to drink is the acceptance of the trials and tribulations, the joy and the sadness in my life. I must also crucify and abandon my pain and what I wanted Him to do with it. I must crucify how I wanted Him to respond to my needs and desires. I must allow Him to do it His way, knowing how much He loves me. I must trust Him.

With such surrender and acceptance, I believe, we enter into intimate communion with the Lord, and He holds us with our cup close to His heart and helps us to drink it.

I believe we can drink from the cup only when we know He loves us. When we have received His love, then, and only then, can we confidently drink our cup,

knowing that in the final gulp we will find an abundance of His blessings.

As I held my cup and started drinking from it, I felt many hands helping me. The hands of my family and the hands of many friends and coworkers united in prayer made my cup feel lighter.

Four days after surgery, the surgeon told me "Everything is good. There is no cancer. It is a benign tumor." My heart filled with joy and thanksgiving. I had reached the bottom of my cup.

As I shared the good news with family and friends saying "God has heard your prayers, I have no cancer," I could perceive their voices changing from anxiety to joy.

When we accept the Lord's invitation to drink our cup, we find that God hides His blessings at the bottom of the cup!

This time I did pass His test!

Living as our authentic self ❧

For He is our peace, he who made both one and broke down the dividing wall of enmity, through his flesh, abolishing the law with its commandment and legal claims, that he might create in himself one new person in place of the two, thus establishing peace, and might reconcile both with God, in one body, through the cross, putting that enmity to death by it. He came and preached peace to you who were far off and peace to those who were near, for through him we both have access in one Spirit to the Father. So you are no longer stranger or sojourners, but you are fellow citizens with the holy ones and members of the household of God.

– Ephesians 3:14-19

We show our God-like nature when we live our identity as a child of God. When I know my true identity, I know I have my Father's qualities. Therefore, love, compassion, faithfulness, justice, and holiness are part of my being. When I absolutely know that God loves me, then I can love myself and love others. When I know my authentic self, then I can see and enter into other people's pain with compassion instead of pity.

When we learn to live as children of God, completely trusting our self and our life to the

Father, our life becomes an expression of our authentic self.

I cannot say that I know my authentic self completely. I am still learning to be and to live as a child of God. I can say, however, that I am far from were I was. I am on my way to my Father's house. One day I will be with Him forever.

Even though I still experience rejection and betrayal, I do not let rejection and betrayal produce the rotten fruits of insecurity or guilt in me, nor do I allow negative thoughts to stay in my mind and hold power over me.

As I open myself to others from that place in my broken heart that God has filled with His unconditional love, I create a safe, open space that invites others to also open their hearts and share their pain and struggle with me. It is in this place, I believe, that God can touch others through our brokeness. Jesus' heart was wounded, and from His wound flowed water and blood. It is the water that purifies us and the blood that heals our wounds. My broken heart turned into a blessing for me and others when I understood who I was in Jesus' open heart.

It is my mission to share my story with others, especially with women, so they too can experience the power of God's love and be an instrument of His love to touch others.

One of these women is Celia. I met Celia in church several years ago. She was young and had recently arrived in Minnesota with her husband and daughter. She was talkative and firm in her opinions, and she seemed to have everything under control. However, I perceived a deep pain from her past. When she was ready, she shared her story with me. One day on her way home from school, she was raped by a young man whom she knew well. She got pregnant. She was only 13 years old. To keep everything a secret, her family sent her to live with one of her older sisters in another city. Ester, her daughter, was born a few months later. Many years passed, she got married and had another child, but her secret continued to be hers and her family's secret. I shared my own story with Celia, and I told her that what God did for me, He can do for her.

Together we shared our life experiences; we cried, we laughed, and we prayed. God started His work in Celia, healing, transforming, and restoring her. Three years later, Celia has become another person and still continues to grow in her relationship with God, with herself, her family, and with others. Her daughter Ester was a teenager when Celia told her the truth. It was a painful time for both of them. "I broke the secret and told Ester everything", Celia told me. "She needs someone to talk to, please talk to her." And so, we talked and prayed and cried and talked some more. I knew that Ester liked to draw and write, so I suggested that she might take time to write or draw her emotions and thoughts.

I asked Celia and Ester for permission to use their story in my book. They agreed.

The following is one of Celia's reflections in her own words and one of Ester's many poems.

Today, sitting in front of my computer, I started to analyze my life, the good and the bad experiences I have lived. I placed everything in a scale. Now I see that the bad experiences are actually opportunities that God puts in our way to help us to grow as a person, as a human beings. After all I have been through in my life I am still here with faith and hope. God sent me someone important to help me restore the faith I had lost. Now, even though I have my ups and downs, I feel closer to God because I have learned that to forgive is to love. I have learned to forgive everyone who had hurt me. That is why I thank God for what I have, my husband, because our relationship is better every day, and because he loves my daughter as if she were his own. My youngest child, because she brought joy to our lives and our home. And I thank God specially for Ester because she has taught me that no matter how hard our life is there is always hope and there is always a smile to make it easier when we are in God's hand. Today I can say that my scale has more good things than bad things, more joy than sadness. That is why I want to thank you, María Inés, for all your advice and for helping me to be closer and closer to God every day. We can never forget that we are better off trusting God than trusting men. Thank you.

– Celia

THANKS

I thank God at this very moment
for every thing that I have.
Although my heart is torn in half
I am still alive,
experiencing all the wonderful things in life.
I've gone through a lot
but that is part of living.
Many people have deceived me
but I've learned to forgive
you can change nobody
you just have to let them be.
I have fallen and I have learned to get back up
I hope everyone knows that I will never give up.
I'm stronger than everyone thinks
I won't just let things happen
because with God on my side
I will survive till the very end.

                                          –Ester

This is one of many stories I have been blessed to witness. Such stories reaffirm my belief that lasting solutions and lasting happiness must come from the inside out. Inside out means we start first knowing and understanding the self. Inside out change is a life-long process of constant discovery and renewal. It requires being honest with self and others, it requires taking time for reflection, and it requires commitment and perseverance. It is a process that creates responsible freedom and effective interconnections.

✿ Honesty with self and others

Rather, we have renounced shameful, hidden things; not acting deceitfully or falsifying the word of God, but by the open declaration of the truth we commend ourselves to everyone's conscience in the sight of God.

– 2 Corinthian 4:2

Be honest. This is one of God's commands. Honesty is one of the characteristics I appreciate most. Honesty affects life, work, and relationships with God, self, and others.

Change requires us to be completely honest with ourselves. It requires us to be open to the guidance of the Holy Spirit. He sees what in us needs to change. Change is necessary. Growth is active change.

He who practices virtue and speaks honestly. . . shall dwell on the heights, his strongholds shall be the rocky fastness, his food and drink in steady supply.

– Isaiah 33:15-16

In my experience the most difficult wounds to heal are wounds inflicted by dishonesty, especially the dishonesty of people we trust. When I am hurt because of dishonesty or injustice, I perceive the other person as an abuser and myself as a victim. I view the other person as strong and myself as weak. Yet, when I come to the Lord and make a place for Him in my wounded heart, I can hear Him say "My love and my mercy are available to all my children. Do not judge and you will not be judged." Then, I can see the other person as a wounded person who is probably struggling with his or her own pain and is unable to receive love and mercy from the Father who is all Love and all Mercy.

When I make an effort to change my perceptions and try to understand or accept the possibility that the other person did not see or know that he or she was hurting me, then God honors my effort and brings me closer to His heart. Out of this place I can honestly say to the other person, "I forgive you. God bless you abundantly with all His heavenly blessings."

As I continue praying for the person who hurt me, God gives me the grace to see reality differently. The issue is not that he or she was dishonest and that I was hurt. Rather, the issue is why I was hurt and how I responded to that hurt. When we purposely change our reaction from resentment and anger to forgiveness and blessings, then the internal change we make will affect not only ourselves, but also our relationship with others and the world around us. Inner changes bring about external changes.

❦ Reflection

In today's world being busy seems to be a sign of value or status. I do not believe it. Taking time to reflect on our daily challenges and behaviors helps us view circumstances in ways we cannot otherwise see. We discover solutions where we thought there were none; we experience new insights, and understandings. Everything seems easier and simpler. We discover ourselves more and more, and we learn how to be. God invites us to "Be still and know I am God." In silence and solitude we hear the voice of God more clearly. In taking time to be in God's presence, we are renewed to continue our journey.

I found drawing and writing helpful in my personal development. There were times when a feeling of sadness from old painful memories overwhelmed me, but I was able to work through the emotions and feel God's presence, love, and peace.

Research reveals that emotions that build up in us create toxic chemicals in our bodies. If we do nothing to get rid of them, these emotions will end up controlling and oppressing us, affecting our health and our ability to clearly see our circumstances. They create confusion and darkness inside and outside us.

Having a special place and a dedicated time for reflection helps me to relax, to separate myself from the voices of the world, and to hear God's voice in me. However, we can pause anytime and anywhere to close our eyes and dive inside ourselves to touch our source of life, goodness, peace, refreshment and renewal.

The more we take time for reflection, the more we see the value and the need for this precious time.

Turning point

> A turning point?
> A breakthrough?
> What is it that is so painful?
> "Do not look at the point of pain
> Look at the new thing
> Look what is ahead
> Stay still and you will see
> You will see the storm pass away
> And the sky clearing up"
> I thank the Lord for the new thing He has for me
> I do not see it yet, but I know it is there
> Oh yes now I see
> The turning point is my trust in God
> Here I am Lord
> I do want to do your will.
>
>   –María Inés Hitateguy

❦ Commitment

You must be wholly devoted to the Lord, our God, observing His statutes and keeping his commandments, as on this day.

— 1 Kings 8:61

Without commitment we cannot change to reach our goals. Without commitment our mission goes unfulfilled. Commitment requires action. It requires that we step out of our comfort zone and start walking in the middle of uncertainty and opposition. When we are fully committed, we can trust that if we are doing our part, God will always do His part.

"Commit your way to the Lord; trust that God will act" (Psalm 37:5-6).

When we commit to becoming our true self and to fulfill our purpose, then we turn our self over to God and become co-creators of new life. We can plant seeds of love, compassion, peace, and hope around us, knowing that God will make that seed grow to give fruits.

Perseverance ❧

Perseverance must finish its work so that you may be mature and complete, not lacking anything.
— James 1:4-5

Our authentic self is the self that God created at the beginning of our life. The process of recognizing, and accepting our authentic self is also a process of discovering, recognizing, and eliminating from our being what is not part of our authentic self. This process begins in the deepest self where we can connect with our Creator beyond conscious and rational limitations.

Jesus' victory over death gave us the opportunity to be a new person in Him.

When we receive Jesus in our heart, and proclaim He is our Lord and Savior, then we become a new creation. Through Jesus Christ, we are God's adopted children. In Christ, God's grace and glory shine upon us.

We are called to be like Jesus, to follow His steps to love and to serve. It seems so simple. Yet it is hard to take off our old nature and put on the new one.

You should put away the old self of your former way of life, corrupted through deceitful desires, and be renewed in the spirit of your minds, and

put on the new self, created in God's way in
righteousness and in holiness of truth.

– Ephesians 5:22-24

Becoming our new self requires effort and persistence. It is a day-by-day process. We may struggle, falter, and lose ground, but we must remember that each day is a new day; God gives us the opportunity to start again.

When we truly want to be like Jesus, then our life unfolds according to God's purpose. We become like Jesus when and if we trust Him and we know He unconditionally loves us.

Jesus endured His suffering because He knew who He was—His identity made public with His baptism —and because He had complete trust in His Father.

I believe the key to endurance and perseverance is faith in Christ. Although life offers trials, tribulations, and temptations, these are temporary. We know that Jesus is with us. We also know that obedience brings God's blessing, which is eternal. Jesus did not stay among the dead. He rose and defeated death. He now sits on the right hand of the Father in heaven.

For this momentary life affliction is producing
for us an eternal weight of glory beyond all
comparison, as we look not to what is seen but to
what is unseen; for what is seen is transitory, but
what is unseen is eternal.

– 2 Corinthians 4:17

Since I now see the hands of God in all aspects of my life, I no longer face pain or trouble by "Why?"

Rather I now ask God "What do I have to learn?"

By acting honestly and in congruence with God and with our inner self, we create responsible freedom and effective interconnections.

❧ Responsible freedom

Responsible freedom is the freedom arising from knowing one's true self and living a life guided by God's words through the Holy Spirit.

> *The Lord is the Spirit, and where the Spirit of the Lord is, there is freedom.*
>
> – 2 Corinthians 3:17

> *Those who live according to the flesh are concerned with the things of the flesh, but those who live according to the spirit with the things of the spirit. The concern of the flesh is death, but the concern of the Spirit is life and peace.*
>
> – Romans 8:5-6

When we are guided by the Spirit of God, we want to follow Jesus out of our free will to the peace and joy of the Holly Spirit. We become free to live a life pleasing to God. This is responsible freedom, a true freedom that comes from deep inside of us.

We often talk of freedom as the lack of constraints, as the opportunity to make decisions without feeling limited by others. However, if we act in obedience to God's words, then our actions become manifestation of the Spirit of God in us. We trade freedom-as-license for freedom-as-salvation through acknowledging God's principals.

When we think, talk, and act within this understanding of freedom—where our spirit is one with the
Spirit of God—then the limitations of the world have
no control over us. We experience true freedom. We
can love even when there is no love; we can be at peace
in the middle of the storm; we can rejoice because the
Spirit of God is joy.

I Want to Be Free

I want to be free, Lord,
Free from insecurity,
Free from the inability to speak up.
I want to be free, Lord,
Free from sadness,
Free from feeling unworthy,
Free from feelings of humiliation,
Free from loneliness,
I want to be free, Lord.

"The freedom you want only comes from living with me. A freedom that comes from learning to live in the present, to do right, to love and to receive love."

I do want to receive your Love.
Help me, Lord.
I want to be free.

– María Inés Hitateguy

Effective relationships ❦

Effective relationships develop from inner commitment, perseverance, responsible freedom, and self-knowledge. From this foundation each person shares their truth and hears the truth of others.

People in such relationships are committed to knowing and sharing beliefs, values, talents, attributes, and attitudes with each other. Such strong, healthy relationships build strong communities.

A strong community is, at the same time, a platform and a setting for fostering the growth and well being of each member of the community. This growth starts in the depths of each individual's heart and blooms in the outside world and the life of the community. When this growth bursts forth in the community, it extends its roots toward other members, the larger society, and the world.

Each member of a strong community recognizes the value of other members because first, each one has recognized her or his own personal value. Once each individual has recognized her or his unique gifts, will see that he or she also makes a unique contribution. It is in the exchange and sharing of each individual contribution that we feel a sense of belonging, of wholeness, of being accepted for who we are instead of acceptance for what we do or from where we have come.

Being accepted and respected for our being—instead of for our doing—creates a respectful, equal environment in which a person feels more at ease to be authentic. This environment encourages sharing. In this environment we learn to look for the good in each other. In this environment we have the opportunity to develop our own potentials, to be who we truly are—not to be who others want us to be.

The body of Christ, the Community of Saints, is the Church and Jesus Himself is the Head.

The same way that our body needs all of its parts to function and to be as God created it, we need the church to support us in our daily walk with Jesus.

Each time we come together to the table to share Jesus in the Eucharist, we can hear His voice saying, "Take and eat; this is my body that is for you . . . This cup is the new covenant in my blood..." And we are reminded that each time we eat of this bread and drink of this cup we are proclaiming the death of Jesus Christ until He comes again.

> *As a body is one though it has many parts, and all the parts of the body, though many, are one body, so also Christ. For in one Spirit we are all baptized into one body, whether Jews or Greeks, slaves or free persons, and we were all given to drink of one Spirit.*
>
> — 1 Corinthians 12:12-13

The Eucharist renews and strengthens us individually and as a body of Christ. We can continue our daily journey with the Lord and with each other in community to be able to then go into the world as Jesus commanded us, two by two, to bring God's love, forgiveness, healing, and hope, which are the manifestation of our true self. When we follow this process, from inside out, we become co-creators with the Creator, creators of our life, the life of our community, and the world. It all begins in me; it all begins in you.

❧ Prayer

With all prayer and supplication, pray at every opportunity in the Spirit. To that end, be watchful with all perseverance and supplication for all the holy ones.

— Ephesians 6:17

Prayers are my daily spiritual nutrition. In the same way our eating habits change according to what our body needs in different stages of our life, I found my prayer life changing. At the beginning of my walk with the Lord, I depended on other people's prayers like a baby depends on her mother to be fed. As I started growing in my relationship with the Lord, my prayers started to change.

I tried different forms of prayers: reciting written prayer, praying the Rosary, repeating the name of Jesus over and over, praying the Scriptures, reading the Psalms, talking to God, praising Him, singing, or being silent in His presence.

We are called to be like Jesus. To be like Jesus we need to know Him and learn from Him. We need to do what He did, to live like Him, to walk like Him, to talk like Him, to think like Him, to do things like He did, to react to our circumstances the way He would have reacted, and to do our best to relate to our Heavenly Father the way He did.

The Scriptures tells us in many places that, early in the morning, Jesus went away to a solitary place. He separated Himself from the crowd to be alone with His Father. Only after He had spent time with His Father did He came back to teach, preach, heal, share a meal with others, and perform other activities.

Making time early in the morning is our first step to develop a prayer life. Before I decided to follow Jesus, I woke up with just enough time to be ready to start my day. Making time early in the morning was not something I was able to easily adopt. I had to make a commitment. I started getting up fifteen minutes earlier, then another fifteen minutes, then added another fifteen minutes. I now rise so I can spend an hour with God. It was not easy, but I was determined to do it because I desperately needed a change in my life. Without this time with God, I feel something is missing in my day.

Below is a powerful prayer I reprint with permission from Jesus Heals Ministry.

> *Lord Jesus, I come before you, just as I am. I am sorry for my sins; I repent of my sins. Please forgive me. In Your name, I forgive all others for what they have done against me. I renounce Satan, all the evil spirits, and all their works. I give you my entire self, Lord Jesus. I accept you as my Lord, my God, and my Savior. Heal me, change me, strengthen me in body, soul, and spirit.*
>
> *Come, Lord Jesus, cover me with your Precious Blood, and fill me with your Holy Spirit. I love you, Lord Jesus. I praise you, Jesus. I thank you, Jesus. I shall follow you every day of my life. Amen*

Jesus Heals Ministry (JHM), is a ministry of healing prayer, in the gifts and power of the Holy Spirit. Members provide prayer teams which listen and discern how to pray for your request, according to God the Father's divine plan. JHM's mission is to assist you, through such healing prayer, to enter into a deeper and more active life in Christ.

In Mark 16:17, Jesus says, "Lay hands on the sick and they will recover." This is what JHM does.

You can contact JHM on Tuesdays, Wednesdays, and Thursdays by calling 651-695-9202.

Being in God's presence ❧

We can be in God's presence when we live in the present—in this place, this job, or this relationship. And, if this is the place we can be in God's presence, we can trust the outcome of this moment.

Most of the time, during my early morning time with the Lord, I just sat, always in the same place. I said things like, "Here I am Lord, I just want to be in your presence, help me to be quiet." To be quiet involved not only refraining from pronouncing words but also stopping so many conversations going on at one time in my mind. I made an effort to stop these inner voices, changing my thoughts by saying, "Thank you Lord for this day," "Thank you for your Love," "I love you Lord," "I praise Lord," "Help me to let you love me." If there is something in my mind or in my heart that I know is not of God, I ask Him to forgive me.

> *When you stand to pray, forgive anyone against whom you have a grievance, so that your heavenly Father may in turn forgive you your transgressions.*
>
> – Mark 11:25

If I have to forgive myself or others, I say aloud, "I forgive so and so and I ask You, Lord, to bless this person with all your blessings."

Resentment and lack of forgiveness interfere with our relationship to God. Once I forgive, I can receive God's forgiveness and I am again open to receive God's guidance through the Holy Spirit, through reading and meditating on the Scriptures. As I continue in God's presence—reading the Bible and praying—I begin experiencing God working in me and in my life. My faith grows and my relationship with the Lord is enriched and strengthened.

At the beginning of my walk with the Lord, I found it very important to have someone to talk to about my prayer time and about what I thought I heard from the Lord. This person is even more important when we go through the process of emotional healing because our own emotions and desires can make us hear things that may not necessarily be from God. I found this spiritual guidance and support in Jesus Heals Ministry.

God asks us to "Pray without ceasing" (1 Thessalonians 5:17). For me, "praying without ceasing" means to have a prayerful attitude in whatever I do and wherever I am. I recognize that without God and His help I am nothing, but with Him and in Him there is nothing I cannot do.

> *With all prayer and supplication, pray at every opportunity in the Spirit.*
> – Ephesians 6:18

The Birds at the Big Bird Feeder

What is it about them that calls me to pay attention?
Oh, I know, it is the color of the cardinal,
Or maybe the red and black of the redwing.
There is another one, how beautiful it is,
But I don't even know its name.
They come and go with so much freedom,
So much energy...
I wonder, how do they know where the food is?
They look so confident; they lack nothing;
They just are; they enjoy the moment.
They go and come when they please.
How beautiful they sing!
I look away from the big bird feeder
Just on time to see through the other window
Three hummingbirds at the little hummingbird feeder.
How, those little birds touched my heart. I love them!
They are so small and yet so strong.
I cannot stop in thinking about how they came to life.
Their way is not much different than the way I
    was born.
They began in an egg, just like I did.
They broke the egg with their own bill to come to
    this world.
I pushed with my head to come out of my mother's
    womb.
I am sure their mom had to feed them, just like my
    mom did.

Then, once their wings got strong,
There they went flying away on their own
It took me more time to grow and to learn,
But I too flew away and I am now on my own.
Why then, it is so difficult for me to just be?
To just enjoy the moment?
To just trust that the One who created us all
Will sustain me the way He sustains them?
I must practice, and practice some more
Just to be and to enjoy the moment,
To be truthful to myself, to trust and to love,
To create in me the freedom of the bird wings.

– María Inés Hitateguy

Peace ⚜

In everything, by prayer and petition, with thanksgiving, present your request to God. And the peace of God, which transcends all understanding, will guard your hearts and minds in Christ Jesus.

– Philippines 4:6-7

For several weeks I was struggling with negative emotions, feeling an anger deep in my being. I recognized these feelings. It was not the first time I have had them, but something was different this time. I recognized that, although the source of my anger was real, somehow, I was aware that what triggered my feelings was much deeper and older than the situation I was struggling to overcome this time. It was my decision either to let the situations control me or to stand up and say firmly, "I am victim no more." I am thankful that God gave me the wisdom and strength to seek Him and to find His peace in the middle of the storm. I was like Peter when he saw the storm around him and started to sink. In fear, Peter cried to Jesus for help. Jesus took his hand and saved him. In Jesus we find the peace no one can take away from us.

Peace I leave with you; my peace I give to you.
Not as the world gives do I give it to you. Do not
let your hearts be troubled or afraid.

– John 15:27

When we feel restless and it is difficult to be at peace, we must pay attention to what is in our mind. Change your thoughts, then your feelings will change. *"Justice will bring about peace; right will produce calm and security."* (Isaiah 32:17)

After years of inner healing and changes, I am finally able to experience peace in my heart and in my mind. I know that what God did in me and for me, God can do for you and for any one who wants to receive His love.

True Peace

My soul is thirsty for you, Lord.
I need your Peace.
Why, how, when did I lose it?
You said "Peace", " Peace be with you".
I have not received it.
My mind is the reason.
It keeps wandering away from You, Lord.
It keeps repeating the stories of painful memories.
Please, Lord, help me.
I am thirsty for your peace,
The peace no one can take from me.
Thank you, Lord, for your peace.
Again, you have won the victory.
Today I am at peace.

– María Inés Hitateguy

Conclusion ❧

Transformation begins when you invite Jesus into your heart and let Him be Lord of your mind, emotions, feelings, will, and life. Such transformation requires effort and determination. To be transformed by God, we must spend time in His presence. We must pray, become obedient to God, and do what is right even when our flesh complains. I am able to overcome my humanity only because I absolutely know God loves me. He is with me, and He never will leave me.

> *He lifted me out of the slimy pit, out of the mud and mire; he set my feet on the rock and gave me a firm place to stand.*
> – Psalm 40:2

God helped me transform myself to recreate myself in His image. When we allow God to flow through us, out of our authentic self, we create new opportunities; we become co-creators of our own future, the future of our community, country, and world. It all begins in me; it all begins in each one of us.

I faced the pain of the past, and found inside of me the person, the woman, God created. I found my true self. Now I am learning to live as my authentic self in the present, in this place. I know it is only in the present that I can dwell in God's presence. And, if this is the place where I can dwell in God's presence, then I can trust the outcome of this moment. He is the perfect Love I was searching for without understanding what I was looking for. Now I can say,

> *I did my part, God.*
> *Now is your turn.*
> *I wait for you God,*
> *For your grace to walk in your way,*
> *For your wisdom to see where to go,*
> *What to do, how to be.*
> *I wait for you, God,*
> *To bless me again, and again,*
> *To be a blessing for the world.*

A year has passed since I wrote the first story in the introduction. Today is the last day of my vacation at a hermitage in the woods. It has been raining on and off for two days. I decide to take a walk along the trail on this cloudy and cold day. I put on my raincoat and leave, but halfway alone the trail through the woods, the rain falls harder and harder. What a blessing!

I love to hear the rain on the trees! It brings God's word to my mind:

> *For just as from the heavens the rain and snow come down and do not return there till they have watered the earth, making it fertile and fruitful, giving seed to him who sows and bread to him who eats, so shall my word be that goes forth from my*

mouth; it shall not return to be void, but shall do my will, achieving the end for which I sent it.

– Isaiah 55:10-11

Along the path I walked, there were many trees that the storm had torn down. Just like my life, I thought. Each storm I went through, at the same time it destroyed something in my life, it helped me to grow. In spite of difficulties and pain, I pressed on and overcame, trusting Jesus for the victory.

I believe it is now time for restoration and fulfillment. Restoration of the true person, the true woman, God created. Fulfillment of all the promises and plans God had for me from eternity.

In the meantime I am enjoying my journey with my Lord. He is the Way. He is my true Love.

> *For this reason I kneel before the Father, from whom every family in heaven and in earth is named, that he may grant you in accordance with the riches of his glory to be strengthened with power through his Spirit in the inner self, and that Christ may dwell in your hearts through faith; that you, rooted and grounded in love, may have strength to comprehend with all the holy ones what is the breadth and length and depth, and to know the love of Christ that surpasses knowledge, so that you may be filled with all the fullness of God.*
>
> *Now to him who is able to accomplish far more than all we ask or imagine, by the power at work within us, to him be glory in the church*

and in Christ Jesus to all generations, forever and ever. Amen."

– Ephesians 3:14-21